A Covered Wagon Girl:

The Diary of Sallie Hester, 1849-1850

Edited by Christy Steele with Ann Hodgson,
foreword by Suzanne L. Bunkers

Content Consultant:
Pamela Petterson, Visitor Services volunteer
National Historic Oregon Trail
Interpretive Center
USDI Bureau of Land Management

Blue Earth Books

an imprint of Capstone Press
Mankato, Minnesota

Blue Earth Books are published by Capstone Press
151 Good Counsel Drive, P.O. Box 669, Mankato, Minnesota 56002
http://www.capstone-press.com

Library of Congress Cataloging-in-Publication Data
Hester, Sallie.
A covered wagon girl : the diary of Sallie Hester, 1849-1850 / edited by Christy Steele with
Ann Hodgson; foreword by Suzanne L. Bunkers.
p. cm. — (Diaries, letters, and memoirs)
Includes bibliographical references (p. 31) and index.
Summary: Excerpts from the diary of a fourteen-year-old girl tell of her family's journey along
the Oregon-California Trail during 1849-1850. Includes sidebars, activities, and a timeline related
to that era.
ISBN 0-7368-0344-0
1. Hester, Sallie Diaries Juvenile literature. 2. Pioneer children—West (U.S.) Diaries Juvenile
literature. 3. Girls—West (U.S.) Diaries Juvenile literature. 4. Overland journeys to the Pacific
Juvenile literature. 5. Frontier and pioneer life—West (U.S.) Juvenile literature. 6. West (U.S.)—
Description and travel Juvenile literature. [1. Hester, Sallie. 2. Overland journeys to the Pacific.
3. Frontier and pioneer life—West (U.S.) 4. West (U.S.)—Description and travel. 5. Diaries.
6. Women—Biography.] I. Steele, Christy. II. Hodgson, Ann. III. Title. IV. Series.
F593.H47 2000
978'.02'092—dc21   99-15274
[B]   CIP

Editorial credits

Editor: Chuck Miller
Designer: Heather Kindseth
Photo researcher: Heidi Schoof
Artistic effects: Louise Sturm-McLaughlin

Photo credits

The Corcoran Gallery of Art, 6; Wyoming
Division of Cultural Resources, 9, 18, 19;
Archive Photos, 11, 12, 16; Western
History Collections, University of
Oklahoma Library, 14; North Wind
Picture Archives, 16 (inset), 22, 23, 25, 28;
Utah State Historical Society, 21

1 2 3 4 5 6 05 04 03 02 01 00

CONTENTS

Editor's Note	4
Foreword	5
A Covered Wagon Girl	6
The Diary of Sallie Hester	8
Inside a Wagon	9
The California Gold Rush	11
Jumping-Off Towns	12
Cholera	13
The Pawnee People	15
Make Dried Apples	17
Independence Rock	19
Wagon Train Rules	21
Starting Your Own Diary	27
Timeline	28
Words to Know	30
Internet Sites	31
To Learn More	31
Places to Write and Visit	31
Index	32

Editor's Note

The Diaries, Letters, and Memoirs series introduces real young people from different time periods in American history. Whenever possible, the diary entries in this book appear word for word as they were written in the young person's original diary. Because the diary appears in its original form, you will notice some misspellings and mistakes in grammar. To clarify the writer's meaning, corrections or explanations within a set of brackets sometimes follow the misspellings and mistakes.

This book contains only portions of Sallie Hester's diary. Text has sometimes been removed from the individual diary entries. In these cases, you will notice three dots in a row, which are called ellipses. Ellipses show that words or sentences are missing from a text. You can find a more complete version of Sallie's diary in the book *Pioneer Children on the Journey West*. More information about this book is listed in the To Learn More section on page 31.

FOREWORD

I started writing in a diary when I was 10 years old. At first, I wrote short entries about the weather, family activities, schoolwork, and friendships. I soon began to write about my thoughts and feelings. My hopes and dreams for the future eventually found their way into my diary. I have kept a diary for more than 35 years. Writing in it is still one of my favorite things to do.

Diaries like Sallie Hester's and mine are called primary sources. Primary sources are letters, photographs, diaries, and other materials that give firsthand accounts of people's lives. They detail the events and feelings people have experienced. We learn about personal views of history from primary sources.

Today, primary sources such as Sallie Hester's diary show us how people lived in the past. We learn about the challenges people have faced. We learn about their accomplishments. Their stories help us understand how past events have led to the present.

Suzanne L. Bunkers,
Professor of English and
Director of Honors Program,
Minnesota State University, Mankato

Sallie Hester:
A COVERED WAGON GIRL

On March 20, 1849, Sallie Hester began a dangerous journey that changed her life. The 14-year-old girl left Indiana with her family to move to the California Territory.

Between 1841 and 1866, more than 350,000 pioneers made the journey from the eastern United States to western territories such as Oregon and California. These pioneers believed life would be better out West. The overcrowded conditions of the eastern United States had led to an unhealthy climate. Disease outbreaks were common, and many people died as a result. Fewer people lived in the western United States, where diseases were uncommon.

Some pioneers traveled west in search of gold, which had been discovered in California in 1848. Thousands of people hoped to become wealthy and make a better life for themselves.

The Hesters did not head to the California Territory in search of wealth. They had money and lived comfortably. Sallie's father, Craven, was a successful lawyer in Bloomington, Indiana. But Sallie's mother, Martha, was ill. Craven hoped that Martha's health would improve in the warm climate of the California Territory.

The Hesters prepared for the long journey. They sold many of their belongings and packed only what they needed into two covered wagons. Pioneers like the Hesters brought clothes, food, seeds, tools, horseshoes, guns, plows, shovels, and axes.

The Hesters said good-bye to their friends and family in Indiana and began the adventure of a lifetime. They joined 48 other wagons to form a wagon train. Members of a wagon train traveled together and helped one another survive. They hunted together and sometimes shared their meals. They took turns guarding their camp at night. They also helped each other care for those who became ill.

Not all travelers survived the journey. Wagon trains sometimes ran out of food, and members became too weak to travel. These travelers often became ill and died. Other travelers continued the journey, but often were forced to stop because of difficult weather. Some of these travelers turned back. Many chose to take their chances and keep going.

Wagon train members helped each other survive. They sometimes shared their meals.

The Hesters' wagon train traveled across 2,000 miles (3,219 kilometers) of wilderness along the Oregon-California Trail. The members endured many hardships. Their wagon train crossed dangerous rivers and deserts. They often went without food or water. Some members died of disease or drowned in fast-moving rivers.

Sallie wrote about her adventures on the Oregon-California Trail. She tells about all her experiences with the wagon train. Her diary describes what life was like for the thousands of pioneers who made the dangerous trip west in search of a better life.

The Diary of Sallie Hester, 1849–1850

Bloomington, Indiana, March 20, 1849 –

Our family, consisting of father, mother, two brothers and one sister, left this morning for that far and much talked of country, California. My father started our wagons one month in advance, to St. Joseph, Missouri, our starting point. We take the steamboat at New Albany [Indiana], going by water to St. Joe. The train leaving Bloomington on that memorable occasion was called the Missionary Train, from the fact that the Rev. Isaac Owens of the

Pioneers saved most space in their covered wagons for food and supplies. But many pioneer families brought along a few family heirlooms as well.

Inside a Wagon

Most of the space in pioneer families' wagons was reserved for food. Hundreds of pounds of dried goods and cured meats were packed into the wagons. Pioneers often brought flour, bacon, rice, coffee, sugar, beans, fruit, and thin, hard bread called hardtack. Many pioneers tied a cow behind the wagon to provide fresh milk at mealtime. Some people even attached chicken coops to the sides of the wagon. Fresh milk and eggs were an important source of protein and calories for the pioneers.

Hardtack

Pioneers could buy fresh food from forts and trading posts along the trail. Prices at these outposts often were much higher than pioneers could afford. Some pioneers hunted wild game when the wagon train stopped.

Most pioneers had a Dutch oven and an iron skillet. They attached a water barrel to the side of the wagon. The water was needed for drinking and cooking. Pioneers also gave the water to their mules and oxen during dry stretches of the trail.

Pioneers brought tools to make emergency repairs to their wagons. These supplies included ropes, brake chains, wagon jacks, extra axles and tongues, wheel parts, axes, saws, hammers, knives, and shovels.

Pioneers packed guns and equipment to make bullets. They used guns for hunting and for protection.

Methodist Church and a number of ministers of the same denomination were sent as missionaries to California. Our train numbered fifty wagons. The last hours were spent in bidding good bye to old friends. My mother is heartbroken over this separation of relatives and friends. Giving up old associations for what? Good health, perhaps. My father is going in search of health, not gold. The last good bye has been said—the last glimpse of our old home on the hill, and a wave of hand at the old Academy with a good bye to kind teachers and schoolmates, and we are off. We have been several days reaching New Albany on account of the terrible conditions of the roads. Our carriage upset at one place. All were thrown out, but no one was hurt. We were detained several hours on account of this accident. My mother thought it a bad omen and wanted to return and give up the trip.

The Hesters' Journey

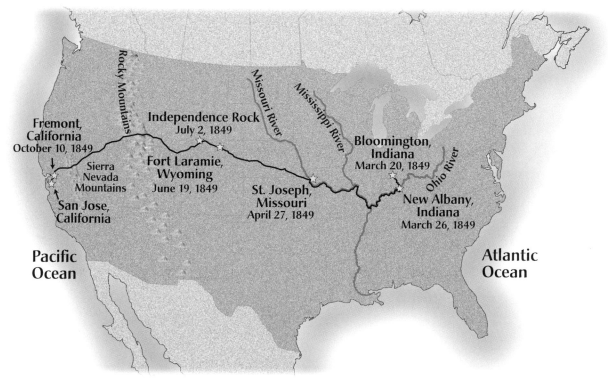

Fremont, California
October 10, 1849

Rocky Mountains

Independence Rock
July 2, 1849

Missouri River

Mississippi River

Bloomington, Indiana
March 20, 1849

Sierra Nevada Mountains

Fort Laramie, Wyoming
June 19, 1849

San Jose, California

St. Joseph, Missouri
April 27, 1849

Ohio River

New Albany, Indiana
March 26, 1849

Pacific Ocean

Atlantic Ocean

The California Gold Rush

On January 24, 1848, James Marshall walked along the American River in the California Territory. He looked into the water and saw the riverbed glittering with flecks of gold. Marshall's discovery started the California Gold Rush. People from around the world left their homes and traveled to the California Territory. They dreamed of finding gold and becoming rich.

More than 80,000 gold-seekers moved to the California Territory in 1849. They called themselves forty-niners to honor the year they believed would change their lives. Most of the forty-niners were young men. They traveled as quickly as possible along the Oregon-California Trail. They wanted to beat others to the gold that they had heard was easy to find.

Many forty-niners who headed West found their fortune. California gold was easy to find with a few simple tools and hard work. By mid-1849, however, most of the easy-to-find gold had run out. Many forty-niners stood in ice-cold water for more than 10 hours a day. After each day of panning, the rivers yielded less and less gold.

Once all of the easy-to-find gold was gone, some forty-niners worked as wage laborers for mining companies or returned home. Some forty-niners traveled to later gold strikes in Colorado, Nevada, Idaho, Montana, or Arizona.

More than 80,000 people traveled to the California Territory in 1849 in search of gold.

New Albany, March 24 –

> This is my first experience of a big city and my first glimpse of a river and steamboats.

March 26 –

> Took the steamboat Meteor this evening for St. Joe. Now sailing on the broad Ohio, toward the far West.

Jumping-Off Towns

St. Joseph, Missouri, was one of many towns along the Missouri River known as jumping-off towns. Many pioneers began their journey along the Oregon–California Trail by loading their wagons onto steamboats in St. Louis, Missouri. From St. Louis, steamboats followed the Missouri River west for 200 miles (322 kilometers) before it turned to the north. Pioneers then jumped off at towns like St. Joseph. The travelers drove their wagons off the boats and started their journey on the Oregon–California Trail.

April 3 –

On the Missouri River, the worst in the world, sticking on sand bars most of the time.

April 14 –

Our boat struck another sand bar and was obliged to land passengers ten miles [16 kilometers] below St. Joe. Having our carriage with us, we were more fortunate than others . . .

St. Joe, [Missouri,] April 27 –

Here we are at last, safe and sound. We expect to remain here several days, laying in supplies for the trip and waiting our turn to be ferried across the river. As far as the eye can reach, so great is the emigration, you see nothing but wagons. This town presents a striking appearance—a vast army on wheels—crowds of men, women, and lots of children and last but not least the cattle and horses upon which our lives depend.

Cholera

In the 1800s, cholera was a common and deadly disease. Pioneers who drank dirty water became sick with cholera.

The large number of people and livestock living together along the Oregon-California Trail often made for unsanitary conditions. People bathed and washed their livestock in rivers and streams. This dirty water often was the only drinking water available to the pioneers.

Cholera was easy to catch and it spread quickly. The disease was one of the biggest dangers travelers faced on the Oregon-California Trail. Cholera victims often died within hours of catching the disease. More than 1,500 pioneers died of cholera in 1849 alone.

May 21 –

Camped on the beautiful Blue River, 215 miles [346 kilometers] from St. Joe, with plenty of wood and water and good grazing for our cattle. Our family all in good health. When we left St. Joe my mother had to be lifted in and out of our wagons; now she walks a mile or two without stopping, and gets in and out of the wagons as spry as a young girl. She is perfectly well. We had two deaths in our train within the past week of cholera—young men going West to seek their fortunes. We buried them on the banks of the Blue River, far from home and friends. This is a beautiful spot. The Plains are covered with flowers. We are in the Pawnee Nation, a dangerous and hostile tribe. We are obliged to watch them closely and double our guards at night. They never make their appearance during the day, but skulk around at night, steal cattle and do all the mischief they can. When we camp at night, we form a corral with our wagons and pitch our tents on the outside, and inside of this corral we drive our cattle, with guards stationed on the outside of tents. We have a cooking stove made of sheet iron, a portable table, tin plates and cups, cheap knives and forks (best ones packed away), camp stools, etc. We sleep in our wagons on feather beds; the men who drive for us [sleep] in the tent. We live on bacon, ham, rice, dried fruits, molasses, packed butter, bread, coffee, tea, and milk as we have our own cows. Occasionally some of the men kill an antelope and then we have a feast; and sometimes we have fish on Sunday.

The Oregon-California Trail passed near the Platte and Republican Rivers, where the Pawnee built their earthen lodges.

The Pawnee People

Many travelers on the Oregon-California Trail encountered the Pawnee people. In the mid-1800s, more than 2,000 Pawnee families lived in what are now Nebraska and Wyoming. The Pawnee built earthen lodges along the Platte and Republican Rivers in this region.

The word Pawnee means "horn" in the Pawnee language. The name comes from the way Pawnee men wore their hair. The men used animal fat to sculpt their hair into a horn shape.

Many wagon-train travelers feared the Pawnee. The Pawnee had a reputation for being fierce warriors. They often were at war with other American Indian groups such as the Sioux and the Cheyenne. But the Pawnee never waged war against the United States. In fact, the Pawnee were one of the few American Indian groups that helped the U.S. government. The Pawnee served as scouts for explorers and military units. They also helped the United States stop other American Indians from attacking settlers.

In 1876, the Pawnee traded their land to the U.S. government for a reservation in the Oklahoma territory. The U.S. government set aside this area of land for the Pawnee to settle. Pioneers could not live there.

Today, about 3,000 Pawnee live on the reservation in Oklahoma. Many of the Pawnee are farmers and ranchers. Many Pawnee on the reservation still practice their traditions. They hold a four-day powwow every Fourth of July weekend. The Pawnee invite visitors to join them in this traditional celebration.

June 3 –

Our tent is now pitched on the beautiful Platte River, 315 miles [507 kilometers] from St. Joe. The cholera is raging. A great many deaths; graves everywhere. We as a company are all in good health. Game is scarce; a few antelope in sight. Roads bad.

Goose Creek, June 17 –

This is our day of rest. There are several encampments in sight, making one feel not quite out of civilization . . . Passed this week Court House Rock. Twelve miles from this point is Chimney Rock, 230 feet [70 meters] in height.

Fort Laramie, [Wyoming,] June 19 –

This fort is of adobe, enclosed with a high wall of the same. The entrance is a hole in the wall just large enough for a person to crawl through. The impression you have on entering is that you are in a small town. Men were engaged in all kinds of business from blacksmith up. We stayed here some time looking at everything that was to be seen and enjoying it to the fullest extent after our long tramp. We camped one mile from the fort, where we remained a few days to wash and lighten up.

Below: Pioneers stopped at Fort Laramie in Wyoming to replenish their supplies. Inset: Rocks along the trail marked simple pioneer graves.

Make Dried Apples

Dried fruit was an important food for settlers on the trail. Dried fruit lasted a long time without spoiling. Most pioneers dried a large supply of apples and other fruit before their journey. Ask an adult for help with this recipe.

What You Need
4 apples (red, green, or yellow)
1 cup lemon juice
small bowl
knife
spoon
2 thumbtacks
piece of string or twine
    about 4 feet (1meter) long

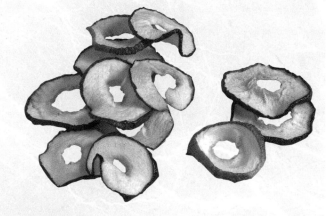

What You Do

1. Wash and dry the apples.
2. Place each apple on its side. Cut the apples into thin slices starting at the top or the bottom of the apple. The slices should be round with the seeds in the middle.
3. Use the spoon to scoop the seeds out of the apple slices. This process will leave a hole in the center of the slice.
4. Pour the lemon juice in the small bowl. Dip each apple slice in the lemon juice. The citric acid in the lemon juice will keep the apple from turning brown.
5. Thread the string or twine through the center hole of each apple slice. To dry the apples, use thumbtacks to hang the apples indoors. Be sure to place a towel underneath the apple slices so the lemon juice does not drip on anything.
6. Allow the apple slices to dry for two to three days until they become rubbery. The apple slices are then ready to eat. You can store extra dried apples in plastic bags at room temperature.

June 21 –

Left camp and started over the Black Hills, sixty miles over the worst road in the world. Have again struck the Platte and followed it until we came to the ferry. Here we had a great deal of trouble swimming our cattle across, taking our wagons to pieces, unloading and replacing our traps. A number of accidents happened here. A lady and four children were drowned through the carelessness of those in charge of the ferry.

July 2 –

Passed Independence Rock. This rock is covered with names. With great difficulty I found a place to cut mine. Twelve miles from this is Devil's Gate. It's an opening in the mountain through which the Sweetwater River flows. Several of us climbed this mountain—somewhat perilous for youngsters not over fourteen. We made our way to the very edge of the cliff and looked down. We could hear the water dashing, splashing and roaring as if angry at the small space through which it was forced to pass. We were gone so long that the train was stopped and men were sent out in search of us. We made all sorts of promises to remain in sight in the future. John Owens, a son of the minister, my brother John, sister Lottie and myself were the quartet. During the week we passed the South Pass and the summit of the Rocky Mountains. Four miles from here are the Pacific Springs.

Pioneers carved their names on Independence Rock near the Sweetwater River to prove they had been there.

Independence Rock

Wagon Trains began their journey along the Oregon Trail in early spring. Beginning their trip at this time was important. Pioneers had to reach the west coast before winter. If they did not meet this goal, they would most likely die from exposure to the cold weather on the plains.

Most wagon trains reached the landmark in the Wyoming Territory known as Independence Rock by July 4. Pioneers named this giant, turtle-shaped mound of solid granite in honor of Independence Day. Thousands of pioneers carved their names on Independence Rock. Today, visitors to the famous landmark can read many of the names.

July 4 –

. . . At this point saw lots of dead cattle left by the emigrants to starve and die. Took a cutoff; had neither wood nor water for fifty-two miles [84 kilometers]. Traveled in the night. Arrived at Green River next day at two o' clock in the afternoon. Lay by two days to rest man and beast after our long and weary journey.

July 29 –

Passed Soda Springs [Idaho]. Two miles [3 kilometers] further on are the Steamboat Springs. They puff and blow and throw the water high in the air. The springs are in the midst of a grove of trees, a beautiful and romantic spot.

August 3 –

Took another cut-off this week called Sublets [Sublette's Cutoff] Struck Raft River; from thence to Swamp Creek. Passed some beautiful scenery, high cliffs of rocks resembling old ruins or dilapidated buildings.

Hot Springs, August 18 –

Camped on a branch of Mary's River, a very disagreeable and unpleasant place on account of the water being so hot. This week some of our company left us, all young men. They were jolly, merry fellows and gave life to our lonely evenings. We all miss them very much. Some had violins, others guitars, and some had fine voices, and they always had a good audience. They were anxious to hurry on without the Sunday stops. Roads are rocky and trying to our wagons, and the dust is horrible. The men wear veils tied over their hats as a protection. When we reach camp at night they are covered with dust from head to heels.

Wagon Train Rules

Each wagon train had its own rules. People who traveled in the wagon train voted on the rules before beginning the journey. Many wagon trains did not allow people to swear or drink. Some did not travel on Sundays. The travelers prayed, read the Bible, and rested on Sundays.

Members of a wagon train sometimes wanted to change the rules during their journey. Members discussed the rule that some people did not like. They then voted again. If the rule did not change, those who disagreed might leave the wagon train and make the trip on their own.

Almost every wagon train was led by a wagon master. The wagon train members usually elected someone in the wagon train to be the wagon master. Some wagon trains hired an outsider to be the wagon master. This person knew the trail well. The wagon master told the group when to move, when to stop, and when to make camp for the night. The wagon master also decided the punishment for members who did not follow wagon train rules.

Humboldt River [Nevada], August 20 –

We are now 348 miles [560 kilometers] from the mines. We expect to travel that distance in three weeks and a half. Water and grass scarce.

St. Mary's River, August 25 –

Still traveling down the Humboldt. Grass has been scarce until today. Though the water is not fit to drink—slough water—we are obliged to use it, for it's all we have.

St. Mary's, September 2 –

After coming through a dreary region of country for two or three days, we arrived Saturday night. We had good grass but the water was bad. Remained over Sunday. Had preaching in camp.

September 4 –

Left the place [St. Mary's] where we camped last Sunday. Traveled six miles [10 kilometers]. Stopped and cut grass for the cattle and supplied ourselves with water for the desert. Had a trying time crossing. Several of our cattle gave out and we left one. Our journey through the desert was from Monday, three o'clock in the afternoon, until Thursday morning at sunrise, September 6. The weary journey last night, the mooing of the cattle for water, their exhausted condition, with the cry of "Another ox down," the stopping of train to unyoke the poor dying brute, to let him follow at will or stop by the wayside and die, and the weary, weary tramp of men and beasts worn out with heat and famished for water, will never be erased from my memory. Just at dawn, in the distance, we had a glimpse of the Truckee River, and with it the feeling: Saved at

Thirsty oxen often stampeded for water after traveling long stretches across dry land.

last! Poor cattle; they kept on mooing, even when they stood knee deep in water. The long dreaded desert had been crossed and we are all safe and well. Here we rested Thursday and Friday—grass green and beautiful, and the cattle are up to their eyes in it.

September 8 –

Traveled fourteen miles [23 kilometers]; crossed Truckee twelve times.

September 11 –

Made eighteen miles [29 kilometers]. Crossed Truckee River ten times. Came near being drowned at one of the crossings. Got frightened and jumped out of the carriage into the water. The current was very swift and carried me some distance down the stream.

September 14 –

. . . We crossed the summit of the Sierra Nevada. It was night when we reached the top, and I shall never forget our descent to the place where we are now encamped—our tedious march with pine knots blazing in the darkness and the tall, majestic pines towering above our heads. The scene was grand and gloomy beyond description. We could not ride—roads too narrow and rocky—so we trudged along, keeping pace with the wagons as best we could. This is another picture engraven upon the tablets of memory. It was a footsore and weary crowd that reached that night our present camping place.

Emigrants faced a dangerous part of the trail through the Sierra Nevadas.

Yuba Valley [California], September 16 –

We are now 108 [174 kilometers] miles from Sutter's Fort.

September 17 –

Left camp this morning. Traveled down to the lower end of the valley. Lay by two days. Had preaching out under the pines at night. The men built a fire and we all gathered around it in camp-meeting style.

September 19 –

Started once more. Roads bad, almost impassable. After traveling for twenty-five miles [40 kilometers] we halted for one day. Good grass three miles [5 kilometers] from camp.

September 21 –

Reached Bear Valley by descending a tremendous hill. We let the wagons down with ropes. Stopped over Sunday. At Sleepy Hollow we again let our wagons down the mountain with ropes. Rested in the hollow, ate our dinner and then commenced our weary march over the mountain. Left one of our wagons and the springs of our carriage. Cut down trees for our cattle to browse on. Thanks to a kind Providence we are nearing the end of our long and perilous journey. Came on to Grass Valley and rested four or five days.

Most emigrants built temporary homes out of whatever wood they could find as soon as they arrived at their new destinations.

Vernon, California [near San Francisco], October 6 –

Well, after a five month's trip from St. Joe, Missouri, our party of fifty wagons, now only thirteen, has at last reached this haven of rest. Strangers in a strange land—what will our future be? . . .

Fremont, [California,] October 10 –

This is a small town on the opposite side of the river from Vernon. My father has decided to remain here for the winter, as the rains have set in and we are worn out. We have had a small house put up of two rooms made of boards with puncheon floor. On this mother has a carpet which she brought with us and we feel quite fine, as our neighbors have the ground for a floor. The rooms are lined with heavy blue cloth. Our beds are put up in bunk style on one side of the room and curtained off. Back of these rooms we have pitched our tent, which answers as a store room, and the back of the lot is enclosed with a brush fence. My father has gone to Sacramento to lay in provisions for the winter.

Fremont, December 20 –

Have not written or confided in thee, dear journal, for some time. Now I must write up. My father returned from Sacramento with a supply of provisions. Everything is enormously high. Carpenter's wages sixteen dollars per day; vegetables scarce and high; potatoes the principal vegetable; onions, fifty cents each; eggs, one dollar apiece; melons, five dollars, and apples, one dollar each. The rain is pouring down. River very high.

Christmas, 1849 –

Still raining. This has been a sad Christmas for mother. She is homesick, longs for her old home and friends. It's hard for old folks to give up old ties and go so far away to live in a strange land among strange people. Young people can easily form new ties and make new friends and soon conform to circumstances, but it's hard for the old ones to forget. Was invited to a candy pull and had a nice time. Rather a number of young folks camped here. This is a funny looking town anyway. Most of the houses are built of brush. Now that the rains have set in, people are beginning to think of something more substantial. Some have log cabins, others have clapboards like ours.

January 12 [1850] –

Water over the banks of the river, all over town except in a few places. Our house has escaped, though it's all around us. Mother has planted a garden in the rear of [the] lot and that has been swept away. Nearly everybody is up to their knees in mud and water. Some have boots. As far as the eye can reach you see nothing but water. It's horrible. Wish I was back in Indiana. Snakes are plenty. They come down the river, crawl under our bed and everywhere.

January 20 –

Water receding.

Fremont, February 27 –

It's raining very hard. A little snow by way of variety. Horrible weather. Received several letters from schoolmates at home.

March 30 –

Nothing of importance has transpired worth putting down. I am invited out so much that I am beginning to feel quite like a young lady. Girls are scarce; I presume that is the reason. Young men are plenty. There was a wedding here a few days ago. Had one of those old-fashioned serenades—tin pans, gongs, horns and everything else that could be drummed up to make a noise. It was dreadful. Weather windy and cold.

April 1 –

Quite a number of our old friends who crossed the Plains with us have stopped here for the winter, which makes it pleasant for mother. My father has gone to San Jose . . . to look for a permanent home.

April 27 –

My father has returned from San Jose. He gives glowing accounts of the place and lovely climate. We have not seen very much as yet of the mild and delightful climate of California so much talked about. We leave next month for San Jose. We are all glad that we are going to have a home somewhere at last.

Starting Your Own Diary

Sallie kept her diary to record details about her life. She wrote about her home, school, family, and activities. Her diary tells us about life on the Oregon-California Trail in 1849. Sallie did not know people would read her diary. She wrote it for herself. You can keep a diary to record the details of your own life. You can write about the weather, family activities, school, and friendships. Diaries are a place where you can write openly about what you think and feel. You are writing it for yourself.

People sometimes keep diaries all their lives. Diaries can become personal histories. Someday your diary might be a book like Sallie's.

What You Need

Paper: Use a blank book, a diary with a lock, or a notebook. Choose your favorite.

Pen: Choose a special pen or use different pens. You might want to use different colors to match your different moods.

Private time: Some people write before they fall asleep. Others write when they wake up. Be sure you have time to put down your thoughts without interruptions.

What You Do

1. Begin each entry in your diary with the day and date. This step helps you remember when things happened. You can go back and read about what you did a week ago, a month ago, or a year ago.
2. Write about anything that interests you. Write about what you did today. Describe people you saw, what you studied, and songs you heard.
3. Write about your feelings. Describe what makes you happy or sad. Give your opinions about things you see, hear, or read.
4. Write in your diary regularly.

Timeline

Wagon trains begin to travel the Oregon Trail.

California becomes a U.S. Territory.

James Marshall discovers gold in California's American River.

| 1835 | 1843 | 1846 | 1848 |

Sallie is born.

The map shows:

Rocky Mountains

Fremont, California
October 10, 1849

Independence Rock
July 2, 1849

Sierra Nevada Mountains

Fort Laramie, Wyoming
June 19, 1849

San Jose, California

Pacific Ocean

California becomes a U.S. state.

Banking giant Wells and Fargo Co. founded because of gold rush.

1849	1850	1852

March 20, 1849—the Hester family leaves Bloomington, Indiana, to begin their journey along the California–Oregon Trail.

July 2, 1849—The Hesters' wagon train passes Independence Rock in Wyoming.

September 1849—The Hesters reach California.

The Hesters leave for San Jose.

Words To Know

adobe (uh-DOH-bee)—heavy clay made from dirt and straw

carriage (KA-rij)—a vehicle with wheels that sometimes is pulled by animals; carriage is another word for a covered wagon.

clapboards (KLAP-bords)—narrow boards joined together to make wooden siding for a house

commence (kuh-MENSS)—to begin something

dilapidated (duh-LAP-uh-day-tid)—shabby and falling apart

emigration (em-uh-GRAY-shuhn)—leaving one place to live in another place

ferry (FAIR-ee)—to carry people or things by boat over water

fortunate (FOR-chuh-nit)—lucky

granite (GRAN-it)—a hard, gray rock; granite is used in the construction of buildings.

haven (HAY-vuhn)—a safe place

majestic (muh-JESS-tik)—having great power and beauty

midst (MIDST)—in the middle of something

perilous (PAIR-uh-luss)—dangerous

pioneer (pye–uh-NEER)—one of the first people to settle in a place

providence (PROV-i-denss)—events for which God is responsible

puncheon (PUN-chuhn)—split log floor

resemble (ri-ZEM-buhl)—to be or look like something else

skulk (SKUHLK)—to move about quietly and secretly

slough (SLEW)—a ditch filled with deep mud

transpire (transs-PYRE)—to happen

Internet Sites

End of the Oregon Trail
Interpretive Center
http://www.teleport.com/~eotic/index.html

The Oregon Trail
http://www.isu.edu/~trinmich/
Oregontrail.html

National Historic Oregon Trail
Interpretive Center
http://www.or.blm.gov/NHOTIC/

Oregon Trail Information Center
http://www.gsn.org/~jmeckel/
oregon.html

To Learn More

Gillespie, Sarah. *A Pioneer Farm Girl: The Diary of Sarah Gillespie, 1877-1878.* Edited by Suzanne L. Bunkers. Diaries, Letters, and Memoirs. Mankato, Minn.: Blue Earth Books, 2000.

Royce, Sarah. *Sarah Royce and the American West.* Edited by Jane Shuter. History Eyewitness. Austin, Texas: Raintree Steck-Vaughn, 1996.

Werner, Emmy E. *Pioneer Children on the Journey West.* Boulder, Colo.: Westview Press, 1996.

Wright, Courtni C. *Wagon Train: A Family Goes West in 1865.* New York: Holiday House, 1995.

Places to Write and Visit

Donner Memorial State Park and
Emigrant Trail Museum
12593 Donner Pass Road
Truckee, CA 96161

Fort Laramie National Historic Site
HC 72, P.O. Box 399
Fort Laramie, WY 82212

Jefferson National Expansion Memorial/
Museum of Westward Expansion
11 North Fourth Street
St. Louis, MO 63102

Oregon Historical Society Museum
1200 South West Park Avenue
Portland, OR 97205

Oregon Trail Museum/Scotts Bluff
National Monument
P.O. Box 427
Gering, NE 69341

INDEX

adobe, 16

Bear Valley, 24
Black Hills, 18
Bloomington, Indiana, 6, 8
Blue River, 14

California, 6, 8, 24
California Gold Rush, 11
California Territory, 6, 11
candy pull, 25
Chimney Rock, 16
cholera, 13, 16
Christmas, 25
Court House Rock, 16

Devil's Gate, 18
disease, 6, 7, 13

ferry, 18
food, 6, 7, 8, 17
fort, 16
Fort Laramie, 16
forty-niners, 11
Fremont, California, 25

gold, 6, 8, 11
Grass Valley, 24
Green River, 20

Hester, Craven (father), 6, 8, 24, 25
Hester, John (brother), 8, 18
Hester, Lottie (sister), 8, 18
Hester, Martha (mother), 6, 8, 25
Humboldt River, 22

Independence Rock, 18, 19

jumping-off towns, 12

Marshall, James, 11
Missouri River, 12, 13

New Albany, Indiana, 8

Oregon-California Trail, 7, 11, 12, 13, 14, 15, 27

Pacific Springs, 18
Pawnee, 14, 15
Platte River, 15, 16, 18
puncheon, 25

repairs, 9
Rocky Mountains, 18
rules, 21

St. Joseph, Missouri, 8, 11, 12, 13, 16, 25
St. Louis, Missouri, 12
St. Mary's River, 20, 22
Sierra Nevada, 23
Sleepy Hollow, 24
Soda Springs, 20
South Pass, 18
steamboat, 8, 12
Steamboat Springs, 20
Sublette's Cutoff, 20
Sutter's Fort, 24
Swamp Creek, 20
Sweetwater River, 18

trading posts, 9
Truckee River, 22-23

Vernon, California, 25

wagon master, 21
wagons, 6, 8, 9, 12, 13, 18, 23, 24
wagon train, 6-7, 19, 21
Wyoming Territory, 19